P9-DXE-461

A Picture Tour of the
SMITHSONIAN

AMERICAN LEGACY PRESS
New York

Coordinated and edited by Susan Bates, Smithsonian Institution
Anne Ficklen, American Legacy Press

Book design by Jean Krulis
Production supervision by Ellen Reed
Production editing by Ann Cahn

Copyright © 1987 by the Smithsonian Institution
All rights reserved.

Published in 1987 by American Legacy Press,
distributed by Crown Publishers, Inc., 225 Park Avenue South, New York, New York 10003

AMERICAN LEGACY PRESS is a trademark of Crown Publishers, Inc.

Printed and Bound in Italy

Library of Congress Cataloging-in-Publication Data

A Picture tour of the Smithsonian.

1. Smithsonian Institution.   I. Bates, Susan (Susan B.)
Q11.P68 1987   069′.09753   86-26612

ISBN 0-517-62609-8

h g f e d c

The Smithsonian Institution

The Smithsonian Institution brings to life the nation's cultural, social, scientific, and artistic treasures and heritage. It is the largest complex of museums, art galleries, and research facilities in the world. Each year, more than 26 million visitors come to the Smithsonian's 15 museums and galleries—from the National Air and Space Museum to the Anacostia Museum—and the National Zoological Park. Millions more share in the Smithsonian experience through traveling exhibitions displayed across the United States and abroad, through *Smithsonian* and *Air & Space/Smithsonian* magazines, as members of the Smithsonian Associates, and by attendance at educational and performance programs sponsored by the Institution, including the annual Festival of American Folklife on the National Mall.

Visitors come to trace the landmarks of flight, to marvel at the complexity of life on this planet, to gain insight into our nation's history and the men and women who shaped it, to contemplate the works of artists and craftspeople from ancient times to present day. And while the visitors explore the galleries and exhibition halls, curators, conservators, and researchers are busy behind the scenes caring for and learning from the national collections that the Smithsonian holds in trust for the American people.

It took the Smithsonian 5 years (1978–1983) to complete the first comprehensive inventory of the Institution's collections. Inventory records showed a total of more than 100 million specimens and artifacts, including postage stamps, moths, spacecraft, elephant skulls, African masks, airplanes, fossil fish, 19th-century American Indian pots, and on and on.

The collections continue to grow, at a rate of about half a million scientific specimens, works of art, and cultural artifacts a year. Most of these new objects became part of the study collections, for only a tiny percentage of the Smithsonian collections is on display in the museums at any one time.

Visitors to the Smithsonian museums are often unaware of the wide array of research conducted behind the scenes by the Institution's curatorial and research staff. Extensive research programs, in fields as varied as paleobiology, desertification, and American art, are carried out in the individual museums. In addition, the Smithsonian has a number of special research facilities. They include an air- and spacecraft preservation, storage, and display facility at Silver Hill, Maryland; the National Zoo's animal conservation and research center near Front Royal, Virginia; a tropical research center and natural preserve in the Republic of Panama; an environmental research center with facilities in Edgewater, Maryland; a marine station at Fort Pierce, Florida; and astrophysical stations in Cambridge, Massachusetts, and on Mount Hopkins near Tucson, Arizona.

Smithsonian research, now well into its second century, is still just beginning. Smithsonian historians at the Archives of American Art search the length and breadth of the nation for documents needed by historians and other scholars for research on all aspects of American art history. Smithsonian curators and scholarly staff have taken their quest for knowledge to every continent and major group of islands in the world and to worlds beyond our own. With support from public and private sources, Smithsonian researchers have a tradition of seeking new knowledge and exploring new intellectual and physical frontiers.

The Smithsonian Institution was born from the generous legacy of James Smithson, a wealthy English scientist. It was created by an act of Congress in 1846 to carry out the terms of Smithson's will, which bequeathed his entire estate to the United States of America "to found at Washington, under the name of the Smithsonian Institution, an establishment for the increase and diffusion of knowledge among men." No further description of this establishment was given.

Receipt of the bequest set off an 8-year debate in Congress over whether the nation could legally accept the funds and the accompanying trust and what a "Smithsonian Institution" should be. Congress finally determined in 1846 that the federal government did have authority to administer such a bequest directly, and the legislation establishing the Smithsonian Institution was enacted on August 10 of that year. A board of regents was created to govern the Smithsonian. The board is composed of the vice-president and chief justice of the United States, 3 U.S. senators, 3 U.S. representatives, and 9 citizen regents.

During the debate on how to utilize the Smithson bequest, proposals were made for the establishment of organizations ranging from an experimental agricultural station to a normal school. Provision was finally made for work in the areas of concern that have occupied the Institution through succeeding generations—art, history, science, research, museum and library operations, and the dissemination of information. In the past 141 years, the Institution has continued to grow and broaden its scope, evolving into the world's largest cultural and scientific complex.

A view of the Castle from the Mall entrance shows the wealth of detail on this beautiful structure. Designed by James Renwick and built between 1847 and 1855, the Castle was the original building that housed the Smithsonian Institution.

National Air and Space Museum

The National Air and Space Museum offers visitors a dazzling array of flying machines and spacecraft. More than 9 million people visit the museum annually, making it the most popular museum in the world. Twenty-three exhibition areas house artifacts ranging from the Wright brothers' original 1903 Flyer and Lindbergh's *Spirit of St. Louis* to a touchable moon rock and a Skylab workshop that visitors can enter. The museum involves visitors directly in its exhibits—for example, using computer graphics to allow visitors to design their own aircraft. Also included are dozens of airplanes and spacecraft, missiles and rockets, engines, propellers, models, uniforms, instruments, flight equipment, medals, and insignia. These items document most of the major achievements, both historical and technological, of air and space flight. Films on flight and presentations at the Albert Einstein Planetarium can be viewed throughout the day at the museum.

Clockwise from above: **Langley Aerodrome No. 5**, heavier-than-air machine (1890s) built by Samuel Pierpont Langley, former secretary of the Smithsonian, astronomer, and early aviation pioneer. View of **National Air and Space Museum.** Model of **Montgolfier hot-air balloon**, man's first flight into the atmosphere (3,000 feet up), by the Montgolfier brothers on Nov. 21, 1783, near Lyons, France. **Wright brothers' Flyer**, this aircraft made the first power-driven, heavier-than-air flight by Orville and Wilbur Wright at Kitty Hawk, North Carolina, on December 17, 1903.

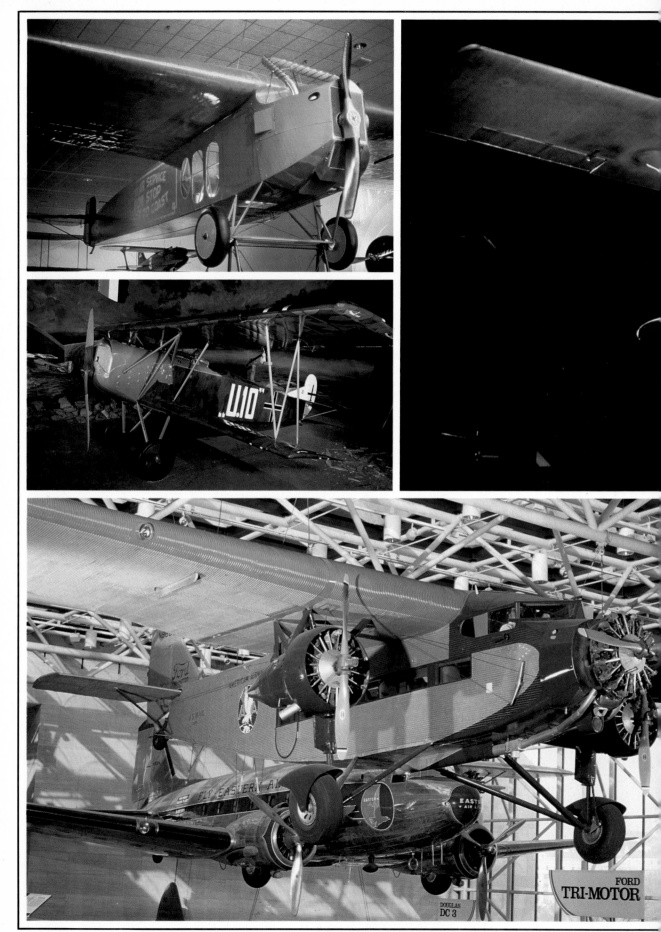

FORD
TRI-MOTOR

DOUGLAS
DC 3

Clockwise from lower left, page 6: **Ford Tri-Motor**, "The Tin Goose," reliable passenger plane of the 1920s and 1930s. **Fokker D. VII**, one of the best fighters to appear in World War I (German, 1918). **Fokker T-2**. This Army Air Service transport was the first to fly nonstop, coast to coast in 1923. *Spirit of St. Louis*, Charles Lindbergh's single-seat Ryan NYP, the first airplane to fly a solo transatlantic flight from New York to Paris in 33½ hours in May 1927. **Douglas M-2**, airmail aircraft of the 1920s. **Lockheed 5B Vega**, aircraft of Amelia Earhart, who was the first woman to fly solo across the North Atlantic in May 1932. **Northrop Alpha**, all-metal frame aircraft of the 1930s built by John K. Northrop.

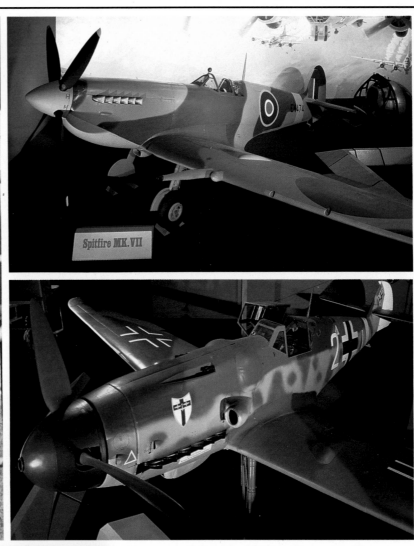

Top, page 8: **Douglas DC-3**, the most significant and reliable transport aircraft in the history of aviation; first flown on December 17, 1935. Within a few years 90 percent of the world's airline trade was carried by the daytime DC-3 and its nighttime "sleeper" DST variation. During World War II, the C-47 and other military versions carried men and supplies across the globe. Nearly 11,000 DC-3s were built and many are still in service today. Bottom left, page 8: **Wiley Post's Lockheed 5C Vega, *Winnie Mae***, the first plane to fly solo around the world, July 15–22, 1933. Immediate left: **Hughes H-1 Racer**; in 1935 oil and movie magnate Howard Hughes built this incredibly fast (maximum speed 352 mph), silver and sleek racing monoplane, which shattered all previous records in 1937 by flying from Los Angeles to New York in 7 hours, 28 minutes, and 25 seconds. Top: **Spitfire**, one of the classic aircraft of all time and Britain's most important in World War II, with more than 20,000 built in more than 40 versions. Directly above: **Messerschmitt Bf 109**, first produced in 1937, one of Germany's standard single-seat fighter planes.

Top, page 10: **Boeing 247D**, passenger plane of the 1930s, modernized and revolutionized commercial flight service. Above, page 10: **North American P-51, Mustang**, highly successful American fighter of the second half of World War II. Lower left, page 10: **Mitsubishi Zero**, the outstanding Japanese aircraft of World War II, this carrier-based fighter was first introduced in 1940. Lower right, page 10: **Messer-schmitt Me 262**, the first jet aircraft to enter service, was introduced by Germany late in World War II first as a bomber and then in its more effective role as a fighter. Top, page 11: **Chuck Yeager's Bell X-1**, the first American rocket-powered aircraft and the first aircraft to break the speed of sound (700 mph or Mach 1.06) in level flight on October 14, 1947. Left center, page 11: **Douglas SBD-6 Dauntless**. This U.S. Navy dive bomber was designed in 1938 and used throughout World War II. Right center, page 11: **Douglas DC-7**. Visitors can enter the cockpit of this aircraft, the first to offer nonstop transcontinental service from either coast. Left bottom, page 11: **Lockheed F-104, *Starfighter***, this powerfully armed combat aircraft flies at twice the speed of sound. Right bottom, page 11: **North American X-15**, first flown in 1959, this rocket-powered aircraft reached maximum speeds in excess of 4,500 mph and reached heights of more than 350,000 feet (67 miles), thus bridging the gap between air and space flight.

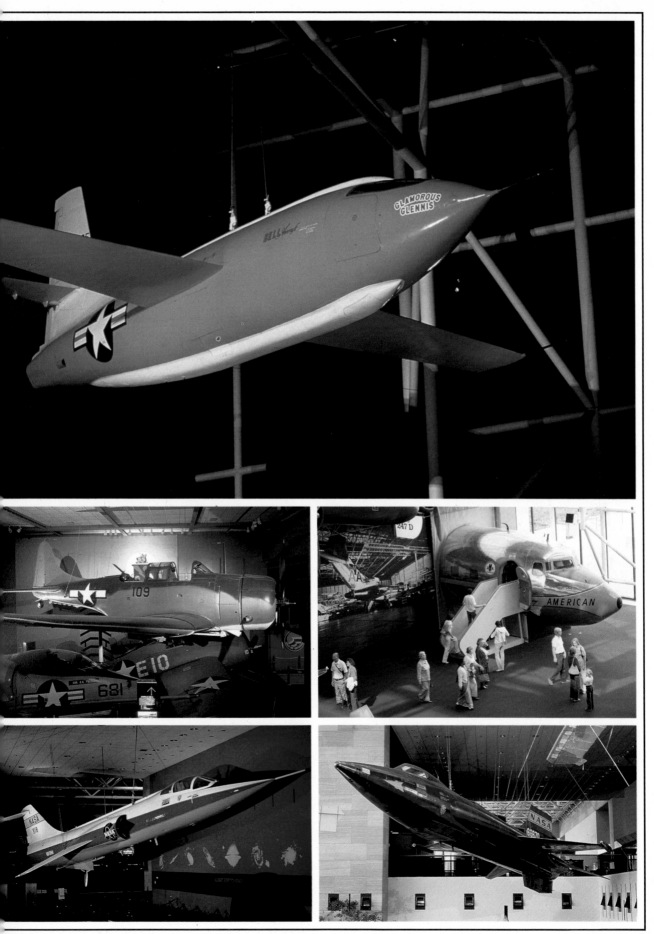

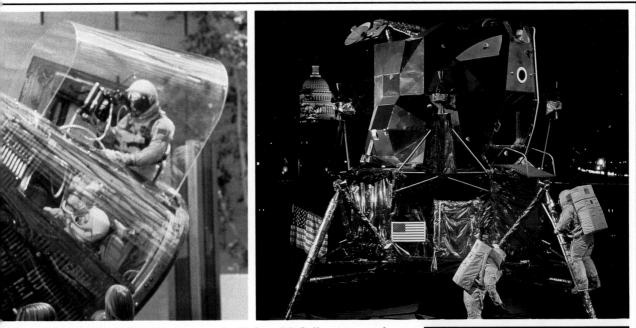

Top, page 12: *Space Flight Environment* by Robert McCall, a spectacular mural in the National Air and Space Museum. Left center, page 12: **Goddard rockets**, invented by Robert H. Goddard, who mastered the theories of rocket physics, liquid fuel propulsion, and gyrostabilization. Lower left, page 12: **V-2 rocket**, German rockets launched against England in the closing months of World War II. Lower right, page 12: **Space Hall**, panorama of rockets, satellites, and probes on display in the museum. Center right, page 12: *Explorer I*, replica of America's first successful satellite (January 31, 1958). Center, page 12: *Sputnik 1*, replica of the world's first successful satellite, launched on October 4, 1957, by the Soviet Union. Lower left, page 13: **Astronaut model aboard Skylab**, the first U.S. space station. Upper left, page 13: *Gemini 4*, from this spacecraft, astronaut Edward H. White became the first American to "walk in space." Top to bottom right, page 13: **Lunar lander** on display with Capitol in the background. *Apollo 11* **command module,** the "base station" of Michael Collins, Neil Armstrong, and Edwin Aldrin on their historic journey back from the moon. **Cockpit of** *Apollo 11* (replica), from which the astronauts monitored their descents to the moon. **Lunar rover**, vehicle used to collect scientific data on the moon in the Apollo program. **Skylab**—visitors can go "on board" when they visit Space Hall.

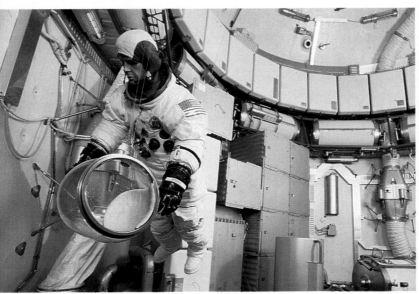

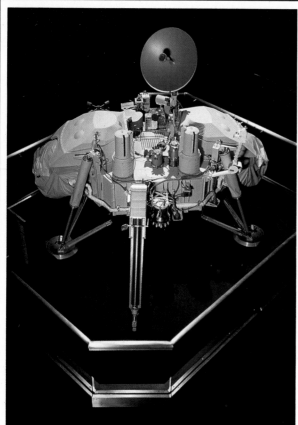

Clockwise from upper left: A proof test capsule of *Viking Lander*, 2 of these unmanned spacecraft landed on Mars in 1976 and sent back important data on the soil, atmosphere, and the possibility of life on the planet. *Mariner 10*, the first space probe to send TV pictures of Venus, also made 3 flybys past Mercury. **Space shuttle Enterprise**, now in the collection of the National Air and Space Museum, shown here being ferried for the last time aboard a NASA 747 at Washington Dulles International Airport (not on view).

Arts and Industries Building

The Arts and Industries Building is a showcase for the American Victorian period, displaying roughly 10,000 objects from the 1876 United States International Exposition, held in Philadelphia. The exhibition was opened in honor of the country's Bicentennial. It is a re-creation of the centennial exhibit. The building's 4 major exhibit halls display a cornucopia of items that captures the true feel of America over 100 years ago: Steam-powered machines, examples of the decorative arts, all types of manufactured goods, and much more can be seen. The building itself is of the period, designed by Adolph Cluss and completed in 1881; it was first used for President James Garfield's inaugural ball. Arts and Industries also has the distinction of being the second oldest Smithsonian building on the Mall.

Clockwise from upper left: The entrance to the **Arts and Industries Building**, as seen from the Mall. Display of **clocks** from E. Howard and Co., Boston, Massachusetts. Stunning array of **tiles**, showing the products of Minton, Hollins & Co., in Stoke on Trent, England, from the ceramic makers and dealers exhibit. This elaborate display shows the wares of the American **E. Butterick Co.** Pictured here is the **rotunda**, the center of the Arts and Industries Building, decorated in the Victorian style.

Counterclockwise from upper left: **Siamese masks,** found in the Foreign Nations exhibit. **Cast-iron bench** with a fern motif is a beautiful example of Victorian design. One of many innovative **machines** exhibited in the 1876 Centennial in Philadelphia, Pennsylvania. The many and varied types of **shoes** made by the Tiffin shoe factory, Tiffin, Ohio. Rice's **flower seeds** and their packages are shown to their full advantage in this arrangement. Over 100 years ago, when this exhibit first opened, **carriages** were an important form of transportation. **Paintbrushes,** artfully arranged, show the diversity and range of this common tool. Examples of native American Indian **totem poles.**

National Museum of American History

The National Museum of American History illuminates the entire history of the United States. Housing more than 17 million objects, the museum displays items that encompass America's domestic and community life, political life, and performing and applied arts. Objects related to science and technology document mathematics and the physical sciences and highlight American contributions to agriculture, mining, transportation, manufacturing, medicine, and other industries and professions. Included in the museum are extensive philatelic (stamp) collections and numismatic (coin) collections. Also to be found in the museum is the Dwight D. Eisenhower Institute for historical research, the Dibner Library of rare books, and an archives center.

Counterclockwise from above left: The exterior of the **National Museum of American History** as seen from the Mall. **Star-Spangled Banner**, the historic flag that flew over Fort McHenry during the War of 1812 and inspired Francis Scott Key's poem that became our national anthem. *George Washington*, by Horatio Greenough, 11-foot statue of the father of our country on loan from the National Museum of American Art, now sits majestically above the millions of passing visitors in the museum. Bottom center, pages 18 and 19: **Teddy Bear**, named in honor of then president and conservationist Theodore Roosevelt, is currently not on display in the museum but is one of the millions of great national treasures that are housed in the Smithsonian archives and storerooms.

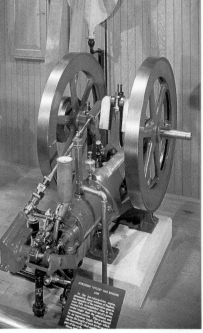

Clockwise from upper left: **Alexander Graham Bell's telephone** was the world's first practical instrument to transmit the human voice electrically over long distances. Bell's first successful transmission was on March 10, 1876. **Atkinson cycle-gas engine**, 1889, a typical machine from the age of pioneering inventions and engineering milestones. **Spinning wheels**—this group represents the thousands of similar wheels that were used to make fibers into thread and yarn in American homes from the 17th to 19th centuries. The transmission key from **Samuel F. B. Morse's** electric telegraph, 1844. **Patent models** showing 6 improvements in steam engine design. **Leon Scott's phonautograph**, the first machine to record sound, 1865. **Bessemer converter**, used in a revolutionary process invented in 1862 to manufacture steel from pig iron.

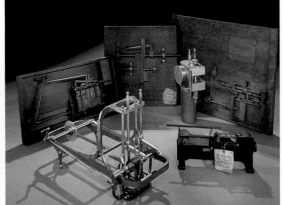

Clockwise from below: **Locomotive 1401**, a massive 280-ton, PS-4-Pacific–type steam locomotive that saw service from 1926 to 1951. **Locomotive *John Bull***, the oldest operable locomotive in the world, shipped to America from England in 1831. **Red velocipede**, a typical early example of pedal power. **Conestoga wagon**—first developed in Pennsylvania in the 1760s, wagons similar to this helped pioneer the American West.

Clockwise from above: **Ship model**, the steam riverboat, side-paddle-wheeler, *J.M. White*, 1878. **Electric car** *303* saw service in our nation's capital in 1898. Richard Petty's **NASCAR stock car**, in which he achieved his record-breaking 200th Grand National Race. *Postal sled*—in northern sections of the U.S., one-man sleds were used to deliver RFD (Rural Free Delivery) mail.

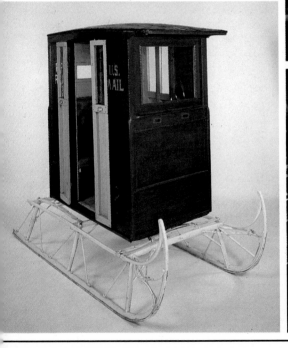

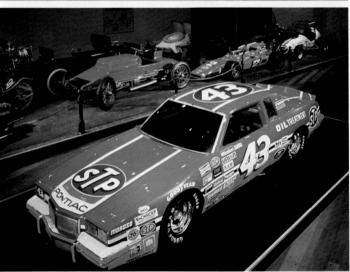

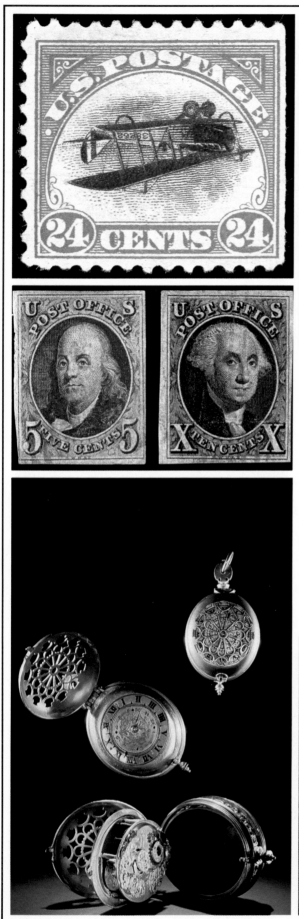

Counterclockwise from right: **1907 20-dollar gold coin**, a beautiful example of the museum's vast world-wide collection of coins and medals. **50-dollar Confederate bill** from the Civil War. **100,000-dollar Woodrow Wilson Federal Reserve gold certificate**, the largest paper money bill ever issued in America. **24-cent airmail stamp**; the printing mistake that caused the inverted center has made this stamp one of America's rarest philatelic collectors' items. **1847 Franklin 5-cent and Washington 10-cent stamps**, the very first U.S. postage stamps issued for general service throughout the nation. A **German clock watch** (shown at different angles) is a beautiful example of the museum's extraordinary world-wide collection of timepieces. **Franklin press**—it is on this wooden press that Benjamin Franklin may have worked as a printer's journeyman in London about 1726.

Clockwise from above left: **Equatorial armillary**, a replica of an instrument built by Tycho Brahe to measure the angular distances between celestial bodies. **Banjo**, an important early example of the great American instrument of African origin manufactured in 1860 by Fred Mather of New York. **Drum**, a handsome red-and-blue parade drum of the 19th century. Mementoes of American music and film, including a famous "Bubbler" **juke box** made by Wurlitzer in 1946.

Clockwise from top left, page 24: Two-manual **harpsicord** built by the Pleyel Company in Paris ca. 1905. "Servais" *Stradivarius violon cello*, made by Antonio Stradivari in 1701. This benchmark instrument influenced the design and sound of all bowed instruments since 1701. It was used in

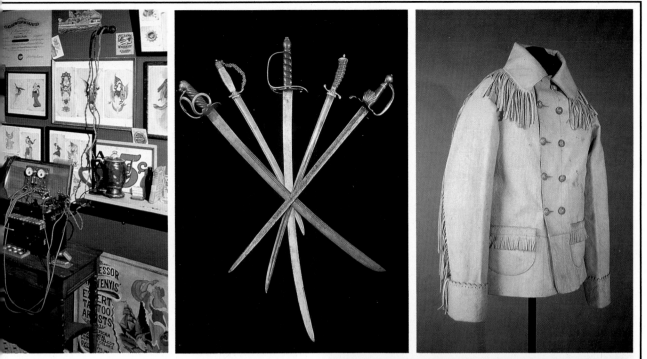

the 19th century by the Belgian cellist Adrian Francois Servais for his concert career. In the early 20th century **tatoo parlors** were found in many American port cities—tatoos had become a favorite body ornament of American seamen. **Swords** from the Armed Forces History exhibits. **Army jacket** that belonged to cavalry officer George Armstrong Custer. **Army barracks** from Fort Belvoir, Virginia, an exhibit showing typical living quarters of soldiers in the 1940s. **George Washington's field tent** used during the American Revolution. **Thomas Jefferson's lap writing desk**. **Election buttons**, detail of a display of over 1,600 buttons. **Benjamin Harrison's dinner plate**, ca. 1890, one of the many examples of White House state china. **Flute** by Haynes, Boston, Mass. This specially crafted platinum and gold flute was produced by the American firm that has supplied thousands of fine instruments to students and professionals since the 1860s.

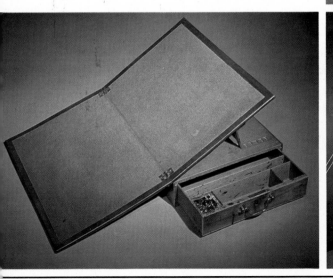

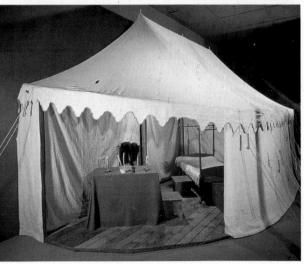

Counterclockwise from above left, pages 26 and 27: **Pottery** display shows the practical and durable styles of the American household. **Pewter** objects illustrate the practice of this traditional craft in America. **1920s kitchen**, a re-creation of a typical Italian-American kitchen of the period. A re-creation of *Dunham schoolroom,* a 1915 classroom from Cleveland, Ohio. **Dollhouse**, a creation of Faith Bradford, depicts an idealized view of a large and affluent American family of the early 1900s. **Ruby slippers**, the magical shoes worn in the American film classic *The Wizard of Oz. Stohlman's Confectionery Shop.* Turn-of-the-century ice-cream parlor, candy shop, and bakery from Georgetown (a section of Washington, D.C.), re-created on the first floor of the museum and now serving ice cream to visitors. Exhibit of a **parlor** appropriate for Samuel and Lucy Colton, a wealthy merchant family from the Connecticut River Valley in the late 18th century. **Bible quilt**, created in the 1880s by Harriet Powers, a black woman who was born a slave, is an important example of design and American quiltmaking.

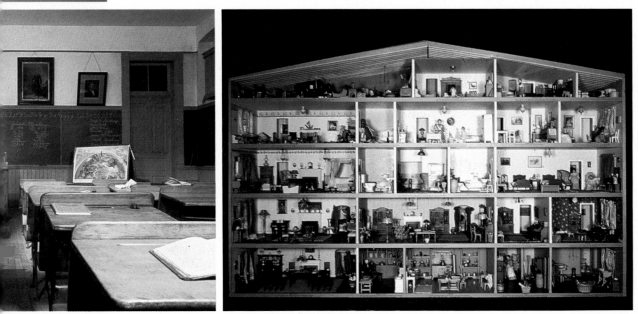

National Portrait Gallery

The National Portrait Gallery houses more than 4,500 portraits of men and women who have made significant contributions to the history, development, and culture of the United States. The portraits displayed are in various media—paintings, sculptures, silhouettes, and photographs. Of special interest is the Hall of Presidents, decorated in the style of the mid-19th century, where portraits and memorabilia relating to all the chief executives can be found, and the Frederick Hill Meserve Collection of classic photographs. The National Portrait Gallery shares space in the Old Patent Office Building with the National Museum of American Art. (Unless otherwise noted, all paintings are oil on canvas and all artists American.)

Clockwise from left: **Exterior**, the National Portrait Gallery. *Martha Washington*, 1796, by Gilbert Stuart (1755–1828), owned jointly with Museum of Fine Arts, Boston. *George Washington*, 1796, by Gilbert Stuart, owned jointly with Museum of Fine Arts, Boston. Top left, opposite page: *Thomas Jefferson*, 1805, oil on panel, by Gilbert Stuart, gift of the Regents of the Smithsonian Institution, the Thomas Jefferson Memorial Foundation, and the Enid and Crosby Kemper Foundation, owned jointly with Monticello. Bottom left, opposite page: *Franklin Delano Roosevelt*, 1945, by Douglas Chandor (British, 1897–1953).

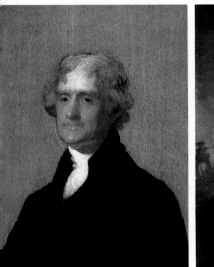

Clockwise from top center: **Andrew Jackson**, ca. 1815, by Ralph Eleaser Whiteside Earl (British, 1788–1838), transfer from the National Gallery of Art, gift of Andrew W. Mellon, 1942. **Ulysses S. Grant**, 1865, by Ole Peter Hansen Balling (Norwegian, 1823–1906). **Abraham Lincoln**, 1865, photograph by Alexander Gardner (Scottish, 1821–1882). **John Fitzgerald Kennedy**, 1966, from 1962 life sketch, by William Franklin Draper (1912–   ).

Above left: *Pocahontas*, after 1616, unidentified artist (English school, after the 1616 engraving by Simon van de Passe), transfer from the National Gallery of Art, gift of Andrew W. Mellon, 1942.
Above right: *George Catlin*, 1849, by William Fisk (British, 1796–1872), transfer from the National Museum of American Art, gift of Miss May C. Kinney, Ernest C. Kinney, and Bradford Wickes, 1945.
Below left: *Mary Cassatt*, ca. 1800–1884, by Edgar Degas (French, 1834–1917), gift of the Morris and Gwendolyn Cafritz Foundation and the Regents' Major Acquisitions Fund, Smithsonian Institution.
Below right: *Gertrude Stein*, 1922–1923, terra-cotta by Jo Davidson (1883–1952), gift of Dr. Maury Leibovitz.

Clockwise from top left: *Self-portrait*, 1780–1784, by John Singleton Copley (1738–1815), gift of the Morris and Gwendolyn Cafritz Foundation and matching funds from the Smithsonian Institution. *Sir Winston Spencer Churchill*, 1946, by Douglas Chandor (British, 1897–1953), gift of Bernard Mannes Baruch, 1960. *Tallulah Brockman Bankhead*, 1930, by Augustus John (Welsh, 1878–1961), gift of the Honorable and Mrs. John Hay Whitney. *F. Scott Fitzgerald*, 1927, by Harrison Fisher (1875–1934), gift of his daughter, Mrs. Scottie Smith. *Frederick Douglass*, 1856, ambrotype, unidentified photographer, gift of an anonymous donor.

National Museum of American Art

The National Museum of American Art is the oldest national art museum in the United States. The more than 30,000 works in the collection present a vivid panorama of American painting, sculpture, and graphic art from the 18th century to the present. Of special interest is a large collection of miniatures spanning nearly 200 years of American art, and 445 paintings of American Indians by George Catlin. The museum is housed in the historic Old Patent Office Building and shares the building, as well as a library, with the National Portrait Gallery. (Unless otherwise noted, all paintings are oil on canvas and all artists American.)

Clockwise from above left: *Black Knife, An Apache Warrior*, 1846, by John Mix Stanley, gift of the Misses Henry. **Exterior**, National Museum of American Art. *Mint, A Pretty Girl*, 1832, by George Catlin, gift of Mrs. Joseph Harrison, Jr. *Children Burying a Bird*, 1879, by Julian Alden Weir. Clockwise, page 33: *Among the Sierra Nevada Mountains, California*,

1868, by Albert Bierstadt, bequest of Helen Huntington Hull. *A Visit from the Old Mistress*, 1876, by Winslow Homer. *October*, 1867, by John Whetton Ehninger. *Agnes Elizabeth Claflin*, 1873, by William Morris Hunt.

Above left, page 34: *Celia Thaxter in Her Garden*, 1892, by Childe Hassam, gift of John Gellatly. Above right: *La France Croisee*, 1914, by Romaine Brooks, gift of the artist. Below, pages 34 and 35: *Achelous and Hercules*, 1947, by Thomas Hart Benton (1889–1975), gift of Allied Stores Corporation and museum purchase. Clockwise from center left, page 35: *Skating in Central Park*, 1934, by Agnes Tait, transfer from the U.S. Dept. of Labor. *Roses*, ca. 1896, by Abbott Handerson Thayer, gift of John Gellatly. *Yellow Calla* (oil on fiberboard), 1926, by Georgia O'Keeffe, gift of the Woodward Foundation. *Illusions*, before 1901, by George Fuller, gift of William T. Evans.

Clockwise from upper left: *Subway*, 1934, by Lily Furedi, transfer from the National Park Service. *The Callers*, ca. 1926, by Walter Ufer, gift of Mr. and Mrs. R. Crosby Kemper, Jr. *Ryder's House*, 1933, by Edward Hopper, bequest of Henry Ward Ranger through the National Academy of Design. *Theseus and Ariadne* (limestone statue), 1928, by Paul Manship. *Going to Church* (oil on burlap), ca. 1940–41, by William H. Johnson, gift of the Harmon Foundation.

Renwick Gallery

The Renwick Gallery is a curatorial department of the National Museum of American Art. It features American design, crafts, and decorative arts. Built during the Civil War, it was the first art museum in Washington, D.C., the original Corcoran Gallery of Art, and was later renamed for its architect, James Renwick. The museum has 9 gallery areas devoted to temporary exhibitions, and 2 of these galleries are used for the display of works from other countries. Of special interest are the Grand Salon and the Octagon Room, among the most handsome interiors in Washington.

Clockwise from above: **facade of the Renwick Gallery** viewed from Pennsylvania Avenue. **The Grand Salon. Hooked wool rug** by Marguerite Tompson Zorach, gift of Tessim Zorach. **Choker #38** by Mary Lee Hu. **The Paley Gates**, by Albert Paley, commissioned by the Renwick Gallery.

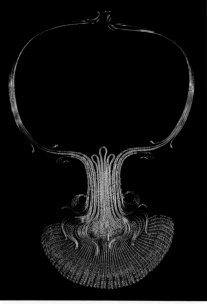

Hirshhorn Museum and Sculpture Garden

The Hirshhorn Museum and Sculpture Garden is the Smithsonian's showcase for modern and contemporary art. Its collection ranges from portraits and landscapes of the late 19th century to outsize canvases and sculptures of the present day. The display and acquisition of works by living artists is an important role for the museum, as it collects and preserves the art of our time. With 900 pieces of art on display in the museum and adjacent garden, the museum attracts more than 1 million visitors a year. The gift of Joseph H. Hirshhorn, the unusual drum-shaped building is uniquely designed for the display of modern art. When viewed from the nearly 3 acres of the museum's open-air exhibition space, the building itself appears almost to be a sculpture.

Counterclockwise from left: View of **Hirshhorn Sculpture Garden.** *Mrs. Thomas Eakins*, oil on canvas, ca. 1899, by Thomas Eakins (American, 1844–1916). *Woman in Raspberry Costume Holding a Dog*, pastel on paper, ca. 1901, by Mary Cassatt (American, 1844–1926). *Family Group*, bronze, 1946, by Henry Moore (British, 1898–1986). *Composition with Blue and Yellow*, oil on canvas, 1935, by Piet Mondrian (Dutch, 1872–1944). *Eleven A.M.*, oil on canvas, 1926, by Edward Hopper (American, 1882–1967). Unless otherwise noted, all works are gifts of Joseph H. Hirshhorn or the Joseph H. Hirshhorn Foundation.

Clockwise from above left: ***Nude on a Red Background***, oil on canvas, 1927, by Fernand Léger (French, 1881–1955). ***Blue, Orange, Red***, oil on canvas, 1961, by Mark Rothko (American, b. Russia, 1903–1970). ***Holy Mountain III***, oil on canvas, 1945, by Horace Pippin (American, 1888–1946). ***Geometric Mouse: Variation I, Scale A***, painted aluminum, 1971, by Claes Oldenburg (American, b. Sweden, 1929–   ), museum purchase.

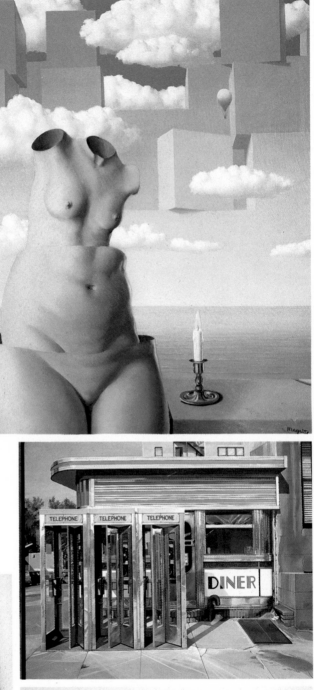

Clockwise from above: ***Rapt at Rappaport's***, oil on canvas, 1952, by Stuart Davis (American, 1894–1964). ***Delusions of Grandeur***, oil on canvas, 1948, by René Magritte (Belgian, 1898–1967). ***Diner***, oil on canvas, 1971, by Richard Estes (American, 1932–), museum purchase. ***Dog***, bronze, 1951, cast 1957, by Alberto Giacometti (Swiss, 1901–1966). ***Beginning***, acrylic on canvas, 1958, by Kenneth Noland (American, 1924–).

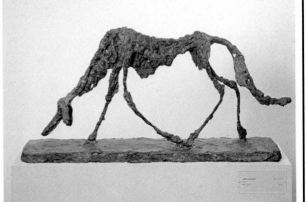

Freer Gallery of Art

The Freer Gallery of Art houses one of the finest collections of Oriental art in the world. The choice selection of more than 26,000 art objects spanning six millennia shows the variety and sophistication of cultures from Japan to the Mediterranean. Also of note are the collections of James McNeill Whistler—the largest in the United States—and a circle of American artists active in the late 19th and early 20th centuries whose works show a sensitivity to and compatibility with the arts of Asia. The gift of Charles Lang Freer, the gallery was opened to the public in 1923 and was the first Smithsonian museum built exclusively to house the fine arts.

Clockwise from above: *Early Evening*, Winslow Homer (American, 1836–1910). *Rose and Silver: The Princess from the Land of Porcelain*, James McNeill Whistler (1834–1903). **Gallery entrance. Peacock Room**, James McNeill Whistler (oil, color, and gold on leather and wood).

Clockwise from above: Japanese painting, ***Boy on Mount Fuji***, Edo period, Ukiyo-e school, by Katsushika Hokusai (1760–1849). **Japanese fan painting**, Rimpa school, Edo period, 17th to 18th centuries by Ogata Kōrin. Japanese pottery, **incense case**, Edo period, 17th century, attributed to Ninsei. Japanese **lacquer cabinet**, Momoyama period, late 16th to 17th centuries.

Clockwise from top left: Chinese bronze **ceremonial vessel** of the type Huo, Shang dynasty, 11th century B.C. Chinese Fa-hua-type **jar with colored glazes**, Ming dynasty, ca. 1500. Chinese **painting,** Ch'ing dynasty, by Chu-ta, 17th century. Persian **pottery**, Saminid period, 10th century. Chinese **painting**, Yüan dynasty, by Chao Yung, ca. 1347. Chinese **dry lacquer Bodhisattva**, Yüan dynasty, 13th century.

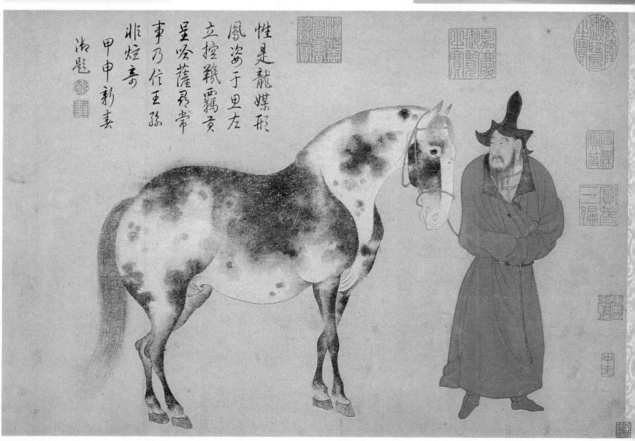

Arthur M. Sackler Gallery

The Arthur M. Sackler Gallery, the Smithsonian's newest museum, displays the fascinating breadth of artistic production in Asia from ancient times to the present through a lively schedule of international exhibitions and interpretive programs that complement the permanent collection. The basis of the museum is a gift of approximately 1,000 art objects, including Chinese bronzes, jades, paintings, and lacquerware; ancient Near Eastern silver and gold; and stone and bronze sculpture from South and Southeast Asia given by the late medical researcher, publisher, and art collector Dr. Arthur M. Sackler. Of special interest are scrolls by important 20th-century Chinese painters, a stunning jade collection and an unparalleled set of Islamic and Persian painting and manuscripts, created in pure gold and silver and in pigments ground from malachite, lapis lazuli, and vermilion. The Gallery is housed in an innovative underground building on the National Mall, part of the Smithsonian's new quadrangle complex.

Clockwise from top left: **The Arthur M. Sackler Gallery** located in the 4-acre Enid A. Haupt Garden. Chinese **carved red dish**, Yuan dynasty, 13th to 14th centuries, lacquer on wood. *Mountain Village on a Clear Day*, Li Shida, Chinese painting, Ming dynasty, 16th century. Bronze type you ritual **wine vessel** from China, 13th century B.C. **Carved jade bird**, Chinese, Tang dynasty, 7th to 10th centuries. South Indian **seated goddess**, granite, Chola dynasty, 10th century.

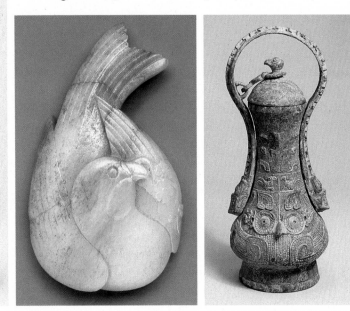

National Museum of African Art

The National Museum of African Art is the only museum in the United States devoted to the collection, exhibition, and study of the visual arts of sub-Saharan Africa. The museum houses roughly 6,000 objects, including a unique, life-size Bamum memorial grave figure and important sculptures from the Yombe people of Zaire and the Yoruba (Nigeria). Also to be found in the museum is the Eliot Elisofon Photographic Archives, consisting of 150,000 color slides, 70,000 black-and-white negatives, and an extensive library of film footage on African art and culture (by appointment only). Combined with a reference library containing nearly 15,000 titles, the museum offers excellent educational resources in addition to its permanent collections and changing exhibits.

Clockwise from left, page 46: **Gold pendant mask**, Baule, Côte d'Ivoire (formerly Ivory Coast). The **National Museum of African Art** located in the 4-acre Enid A. Haupt Garden. **Harp**, Zande, Zaire. **Wood figure**, Kongo (Yombe), Zaire. **Figure of seated male and female (Akua'ba)**, Akan peoples, Ghana. Clockwise from upper left, page 47: **Memorial grave figure** of a colonial officer, Bamun, Cameroon, gift of E.A.J. Hall and J. A. Friede. **Koro Ache headdress** from northern Nigeria. **Nigerian vessel** with chameleons, ca. 1668. **Commemorative head**, Benin, Nigeria, ca. 15th to 16th century. **Terra-cotta pipe**, Shilluk, Sudan.

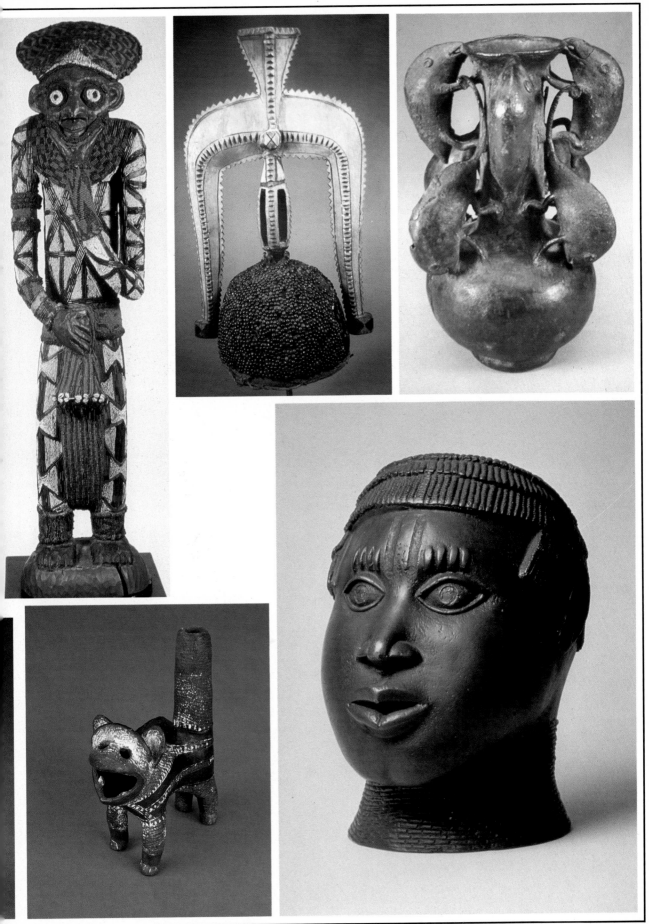

Anacostia Museum

The Anacostia Museum opened to the public in 1967 as the first of its kind in the nation. Created in response to organized community efforts to establish a museum in the historic Anacostia section of Southeast Washington, the museum provides a wide range of changing exhibitions and programs that are related to Afro-American culture and history. A research, design, and production staff creates all the museum's exhibits, and the museum houses reference materials for use by scholars. The museum is located at 1901 Fort Place, S.E. in Fort Stanton Park, site of a Civil War fort erected to protect the Navy Yard.

Clockwise from above: The new quarters for the **Anacostia Museum**. Bronze bust of **Fredrick Douglass** by Ed Dwight. **Tye-dying** activity during Annual Family Day. **Sojourner Truth doll** by Cecilia Rothman.

Cooper-Hewitt Museum

The Cooper-Hewitt Museum, located in New York City, is the only museum in the United States devoted exclusively to the study and exhibition of historical and contemporary design. The collections span more than 3,000 years and are supported by one of the finest specialized libraries in the country. The permanent collection of the Cooper-Hewitt contains more than 300,000 decorative art objects, including textiles, furniture, ceramics, glass, architectural ornaments, metalwork, woodwork, drawings, and prints. Of special note are the museum's design drawings representing Europe and the United States and an outstanding wallpaper collection. The Cooper-Hewitt reference center contains more than 35,000 books, a large picture collection, and archives on color, pattern, symbols, advertising, and industrial design. The museum is located in the Carnegie Mansion, an elegant Georgian Revival home built by Andrew Carnegie.

Clockwise from below: The **Cooper-Hewitt Museum**. Manufacture Impériale de Sèvres, French, **cabaret service**, ca. 1813, gift of Mrs. Katrina H. Becker in memory of her parents, Mr. and Mrs. Charles V. Hickox. Emile Gallé, French, **figure of a dog**, ca. 1870, anonymous bequest. William Morris, English, **pair of curtains**, tulip and rose design, gift of Harvey Smith. **French wallpaper dado**, ca. 1820, gift of Josephine Howell.

National Museum of Natural History

The National Museum of Natural History is the country's largest research museum and contains one of the world's biggest and most valuable scientific collections. The collections include about 118 million animals, plants, fossil organisms, rocks, minerals, and cultural artifacts. The museum is also the official repository for the extensive scientific collections cquired by U.S. government expeditions. About 7 million people visit the museum every year, enjoying both the permanent and traveling exhibitions in the museum's 30 exhibit halls. Visitors can view exhibits on such diverse subjects as the Ice Age, the rise of Western civilization, the geological history of the earth and moon, dinosaurs and other extinct animals and plants, gems and minerals, meteorites, and much more. Also of note are the live Insect Zoo, the Discovery Room, and the Naturalist Center.

Counterclockwise from left: **National Museum of Natural History** as seen from the entrance on the Mall—"Uncle Beazley," a fiberglass model of **Triceratops**, can be seen in the lower left corner. **Bengal tiger**, at 11-feet, 1-inch, weighing in at 857 pounds, believed to be the largest tiger ever taken in India. Front view of a **walrus**, a polar marine animal that can weigh as much as 3,000 pounds when full grown. A diorama of **mountain goats** foraging in the Rockies. Not a true goat, these animals belong to a special group of goat-antelopes. This surefooted animal is completely at home in the mountains of the northwest United States and Canada. An **African bush elephant**, the largest land animal on earth today.

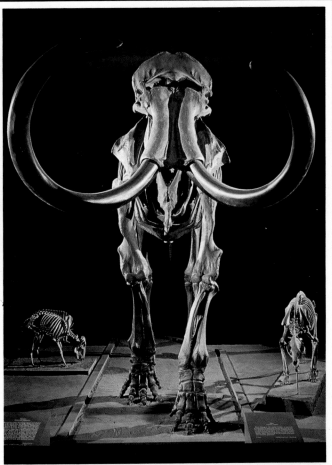

Counterclockwise from upper left: A **blue whale** displayed in the hall of sea life is a life-size, 92-foot replica of the largest animal species on earth today. A view of **moose** in their natural North American habitat. Spectacular view of the museum's four-storied **rotunda**, and the **African bush elephant** in the center. Woman poses (for scale) inside the enormous reconstructed jaws and actual fossil teeth of an extinct 4.5 million-year-old **great white shark**. Skeleton of a **woolly mammoth** on display in the Ice Age hall. Skeleton of a **sabertoothed tiger** of 14,000 years ago from the tar pits of Rancho La Brea, California.

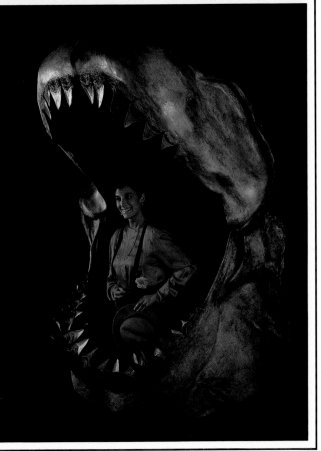

Counterclockwise: A skeleton of **Stego-saurus** from the Jurassic Period. *Stego-saurus* was a large, plated dinosaur that roamed in the area that is now Colorado, Utah, and Wyoming. **Quetzalcoatlus northropi**, a life-size replica of a **ptero-saur**, a flying reptile of the Mesozoic Era. The well-loved model of **Triceratops**, nicknamed "Uncle Beazley," that stands outside the museum's mall entrance. A **diorama of the Jurassic Period** 135 million years ago, showing the plant and animal life of the time. **Skeletal view of Triceratops**, a dinosaur of the Cretaceous Period. The average *triceratops* weighed 7 tons and was 20 feet long, and though fierce-looking was actually a plant eater.

Clockwise from upper right: A grouping of **treasures from Troy**, representative of the museum's vast anthropological collections that catalog cultures from all over the world. Ancient **bronze dagger**. A reconstruction of a **Neanderthal burial** as seen in Regourdou Cave in southern France, roughly 70,000 years ago—the burial rites reflected here show Neanderthal man to be more advanced in his culture than popularly believed. This linen-wrapped **cat mummy** was embalmed by ancient Egyptians to accompany its owner into the afterlife.

Counterclockwise: **Kwakiutl Indian mask**, representing a raven, is from British Columbia, made in 1894. A grouping of **African artifacts**, showing the diversity and richness of their craftsmanship. This **Arapaho tepee** was displayed at the Philadelphia Centennial Exposition of 1876 and it is constructed of 14 buffalo hides laced together.

Clockwise from upper left, page 57: A **Zuñi pot** collected in the 1880s. **Yei rug** from the Navajo. Sioux Indian **eagle-feather headdress**, ca. 1880, with ermine tails, horsehair, and beadwork. A diorama depicting a traditional scene of **Polar Eskimo life** in the Arctic. A heavily fringed **Plains Indian garment**.

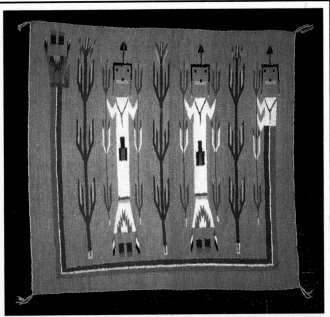

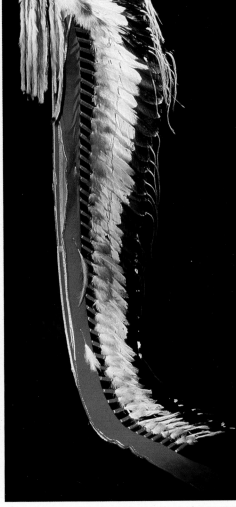

POLAR ESKIMO
THE NORTHERNMOST PEOPLE OF THE WORLD

Counterclockwise from above: **Birdwing butterfly**, from the museum's extensive collection. **Orange-knee tarantula** from central South America, a resident of the Insect Zoo. **Cone-head grasshopper**, from Central America. **Precious wentletrap**, a marine snail shell from the Pescadores, Taiwan. A visitor in the **Discovery Room**, where people can touch and explore natural history objects, investigates a stuffed crocodile. **Diamond earrings**, that are believed to have belonged to Marie Antoinette, queen of France in the 1700s. **Warner crystal ball** weighing 106¾ pounds was cut from a large quartz crystal. A piece of **smithsonite**, the ore named for James Smithson, founder of the Smithsonian Institution. The famous and stunning **Hope Diamond**, named after Philip Hope, a British collector—the stone weighs 45.5 carats, making it the largest blue diamond on public display in the world. It is also noted for its deep color and flawless clarity. Cross-section of a piece of **malachite**. The **Spanish Inquisition necklace**, crafted more than 300 years ago using emeralds from Colombia and diamonds from India. Grouping showing the range and diversity of **crystals**.

National Zoological Park

The National Zoological Park, established in 1889, contains over 400 species, roughly 3,000 animals from all over the world. Nearly 25 percent of the species are considered rare or endangered, and the National Zoo has received worldwide recognition for its care, exhibition, and conservation of endangered and exotic animals. The zoo also takes pride in its projects that have led to better care of animals in captivity and a current project in which the endangered golden lion tamarin is being bred and then returned to its native habitat in Brazil. Famous residents at the zoo have included Smokey the Bear, who became a national symbol for fire protection, and currently, the giant pandas Ling-Ling and Hsing-Hsing, gifts from the People's Republic of China.

Counterclockwise from left: Hsing-Hsing male giant panda, a 1972 gift from the People's Republic of China. Native to Africa and India, these **male and female lions** can be seen roaming in one of the zoo's many open-air exhibition areas. An **adult pampas cat** stalks through the undergrowth. **Infant and adult giraffes**, examples of the tallest quadrupeds in the world. A **Kodiak bear**, one of the many types of bears to be found at the zoo. This bear is found on Kodiak Island, Alaska.

Counterclockwise from upper left: **Red kangaroos** in one of the large enclosures that offer unobstructed views for visitors and plenty of space for the animals. **Sable antelope**, native to Africa. A **black bear**, the most common bear in the United States—the black bear was the model for the original teddy bear. **Boa constrictor**, native to tropical North and South America, noted for its ability to suffocate its prey in its coils, but this snake is safe for viewing. The **slow loris** is a nocturnal, tree-living primate found in southeastern Asia. **Baby Asiatic elephant**, a popular zoo resident. **Armadillos** are found in South America and southern North America. Their armorlike plates are for protection.

Smithsonian museums in Washington are open every day of the year, with the exception of December 25, and have free admission. Unless otherwise noted, hours are 10:00 A.M. to 5:30 P.M.

Smithsonian Institution Building (Castle)
1000 Jefferson Drive, S.W.
Visitor Information and Associates' Reception Center,
 Crypt Room with tomb of James Smithson, Woodrow
 Wilson Center

National Air and Space Museum
Independence Avenue at 6th Street, S.W.
Museum Shop, Spacearium Shop, Shuttle Shop, Films
 and Planetarium Shows, Cafeteria, Outdoor Café
 (seasonal)

Arts and Industries Building
Jefferson Drive at 9th Street, S.W.
Museum Shop, Discovery Theater

National Museum of American History
Constitution Avenue between 12th and 14th Streets,
 N.W.
Museum Shop and Bookstore, Smithsonian Post
 Office, Cafeteria, Palm Court (ice cream parlor)

National Portrait Gallery
8th and F Streets, N.W.
Museum Shop, Cafeteria

National Museum of American Art
8th and G Streets, N.W.
Museum Shop, Cafeteria

Renwick Gallery
Pennsylvania Avenue at 17th Street
Museum Shop

Hirshhorn Museum and Sculpture Garden
Independence Avenue at 8th Street, S.W.
Museum Shop, Outdoor Café (seasonal)

Freer Gallery of Art
Jefferson Drive at 12th Street, S.W.
Museum Shop

Arthur M. Sackler Gallery
1050 Independence Avenue, S.W.
Museum Shop

National Museum of African Art
950 Independence Avenue, S.W.
Museum Shop

Anacostia Museum
1901 Fort Place, S.E.
Hours: 10:00 A.M. to 5:00 P.M.

Cooper-Hewitt Museum
2 East 91st Street, New York, New York
Tuesday, 10:00 A.M. to 9:00 P.M.; Wednesday through
 Saturday, 10:00 A.M. to 5:00 P.M.; Sunday, noon to 5:00
 P.M.; Closed Monday and major holidays. Museum
 Shop. Admission charged.

National Museum of Natural History
Constitution Avenue at 10th Street, N.W.
Museum Shop, Cafeteria, Smithsonian Associates'
Dining Room, Discovery Room, Naturalist Center,
Evans Gallery

National Zoological Park
Entrances: Connecticut Avenue, N.W. (3000 block
 between Cathedral Avenue and Devonshire Place);
 Harvard Street and Adams Mill Road intersection;
 Beach Drive in Rock Creek Park
Winter hours:
 Grounds: 8:00 A.M. to 6:00 P.M.
 Buildings: 9:00 A.M. to 4:30 P.M.
Summer hours:
 Grounds: 8:00 A.M. to 8:00 P.M.
 Buildings: 9:00 A.M. to 6:00 P.M.
Gift Shop, Parking Facilities, Food and Picnic Facilities

The Smithsonian Facilities also include:
Paul E. Garber Preservation, Restoration and Storage
 Facility
Smithsonian Astrophysical Observatory
Smithsonian Marine Station
Smithsonian Environmental Research Center
Smithsonian Tropical Research Institute
Archives of American Art
Conservation and Research Center of the National
 Zoo
Barney Studio House
S. Dillon Ripley Center
International Center Galley

For further information, write or call:
Visitor Information and Associates' Reception Center
Smithsonian Institution
Washington, D.C. 20560
202-357-2700; TDD for hearing impaired, 202-357-1729

Photo Credits: National Portrait Gallery: Eugene Mantie and
Roland White

A colorful overview of the Smithsonian **museum shop** in the National Air and Space Museum. The 15 museum shops in 9 museums offer an exciting array of gifts, reproductions, books, postcards, and other items that reflect the unique character of each host museum.